Dedicated to my students
-Mrs. Dorcely

This book belongs to:

_____

We are getting ready for
the garden trip to celebrate Earth Day.
Ms. D turns the classroom into a garden!

Stamp or check

SUPPLIES

Ms. D gives each student a bag with supplies to record what is growing in the garden.

Each student gets a magnifying glass
to look at what is growing in the garden.

Check what is growing in the garden!

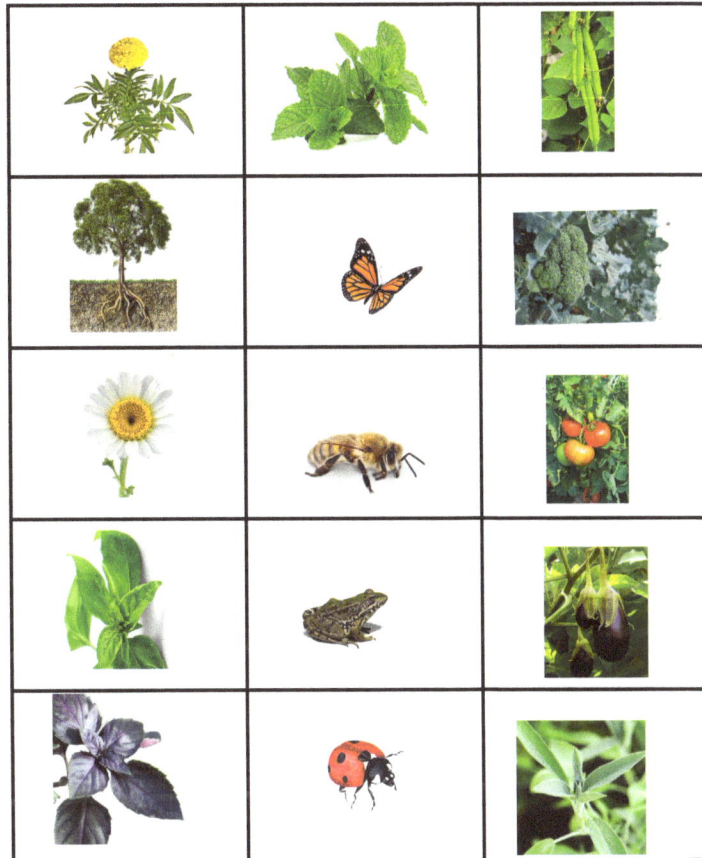

Each student gets a chart with plants and animals.

Each student gets a stamp.

Each student gets a pencil.

At the garden, Ms. D asks the students,
"What is growing in the garden?"

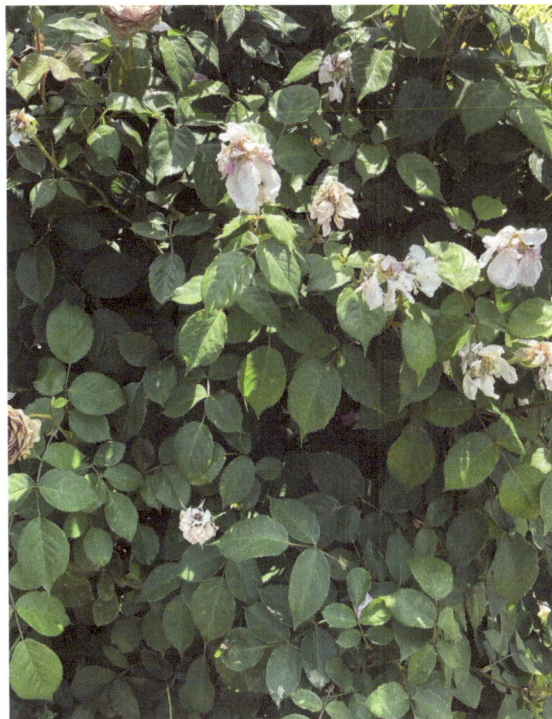

The students say,
"Flowers are growing in the garden."

This is a flower.

petal

petal

A flower has petals.

stem

A flower has a stem.

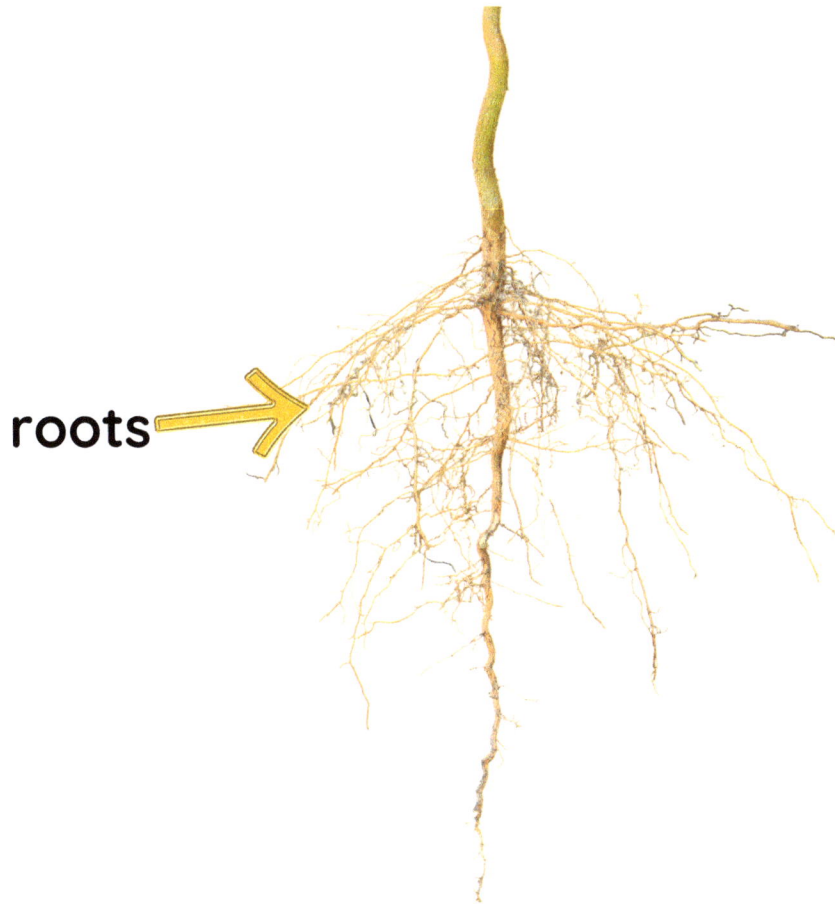

roots

A flower has roots.

leaves →

A flower has leaves.

This is a tulip.

This is a rose.

This is a carnation.

This is a sunflower.

This is a lily.

This is a marigold.

This is a daisy.

Some students say, "tall trees and short trees are growing in the garden."

This is a tree.

roots

A tree has roots.

trunk →

A tree has a trunk.

branches

A tree has branches.

leaves

A tree has leaves.

The students chant!

A tree has many parts,
many parts, many parts

A tree has many parts,
I can name them all!

Roots, roots, roots
Trunk, trunk, trunk
Branches, branches, branches
Leaves, leaves, leaves
I can name them all!

It is your turn to visit a garden
to celebrate Earth Day.

Get your tools!

Check what you see in the garden rose tulip carnation sunflower lily	**chart**
	stamp
	bag
	magnifying glass
	pencil

Adaptable Photos and Words

	petals 	**petals**
	leaves 	**leaves**
	stem 	**stem**
	roots 	**roots**
	flower 	**flower**

Adaptable Photos and Words

	rose	**rose**
	tulip	**tulip**
	carnation	**carnation**
	sunflower	**sunflower**
	lily	**lily**

Adaptable Photos and Words

	marigold	marigold
	daisy	daisy
	flowers	flowers
	garden	garden
	garden	garden

Adaptable Photos and Words

	branches 	**branches**
	roots 	**roots**
	leaves 	**leaves**
	trunk 	**trunk**
	tree 	**tree**

Activities

What do you see in the garden?

Check off what you see in the garden

	rose	
	tulip	
	carnation	
	sunflower	
	lily	

Check off what you see in the garden

	marigold	
	daisy	
	flowers	
	garden	

Check off what you see in the garden

	branches	
	roots	
	leaves	
	trunk	
	tree	

Draw and label what you see in the garden

Draw and write
what you see in the garden

Write about what you see in the garden

_____

_____

_____

_____

_____

_____

_____

_____

_____

_____

_____

_____

_____

A flower has

_____

_____

_____

_____

petals

leaves

roots

stem

A flower has

petals **leaves** **roots** **stem**

Draw a flower and label the parts

A tree has

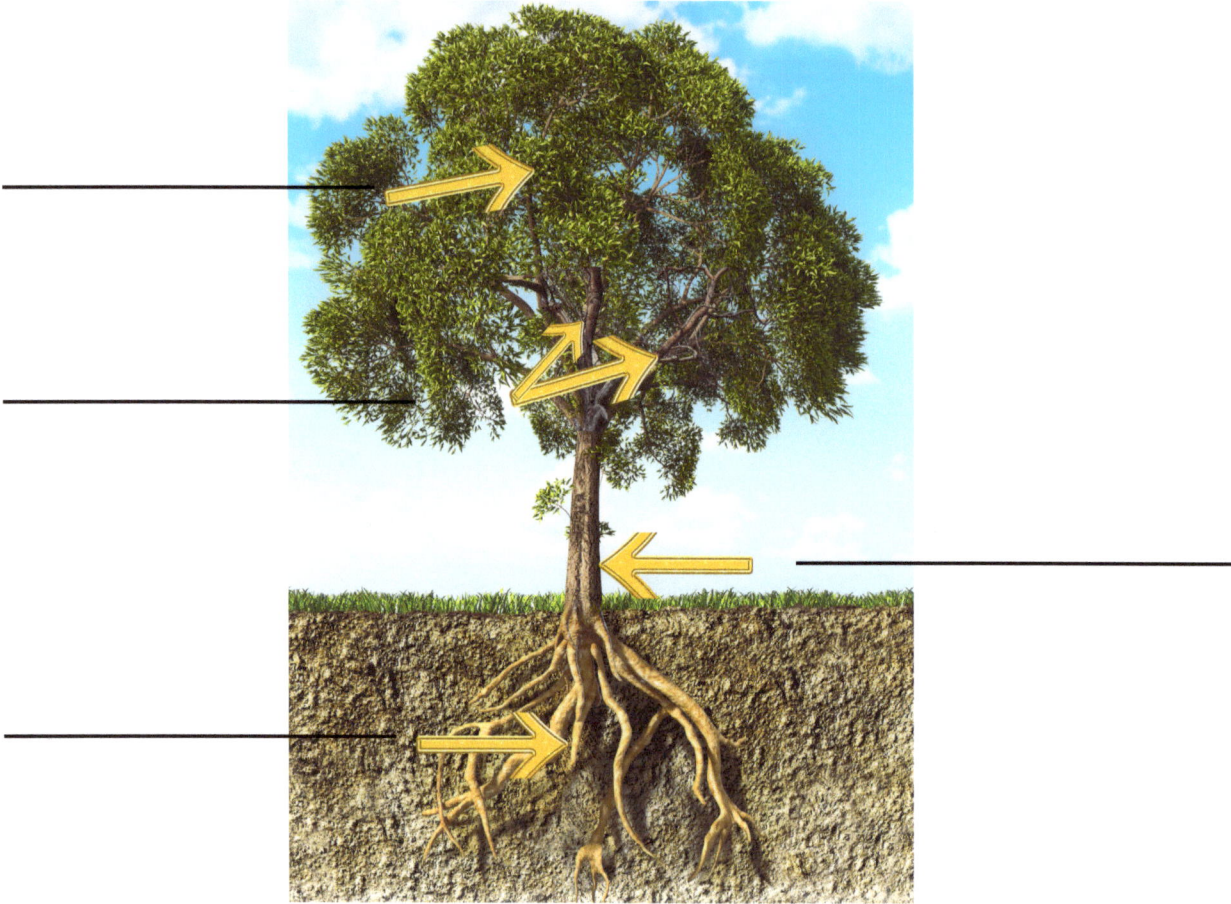

roots **leaves** **branches** **trunk**

A tree has

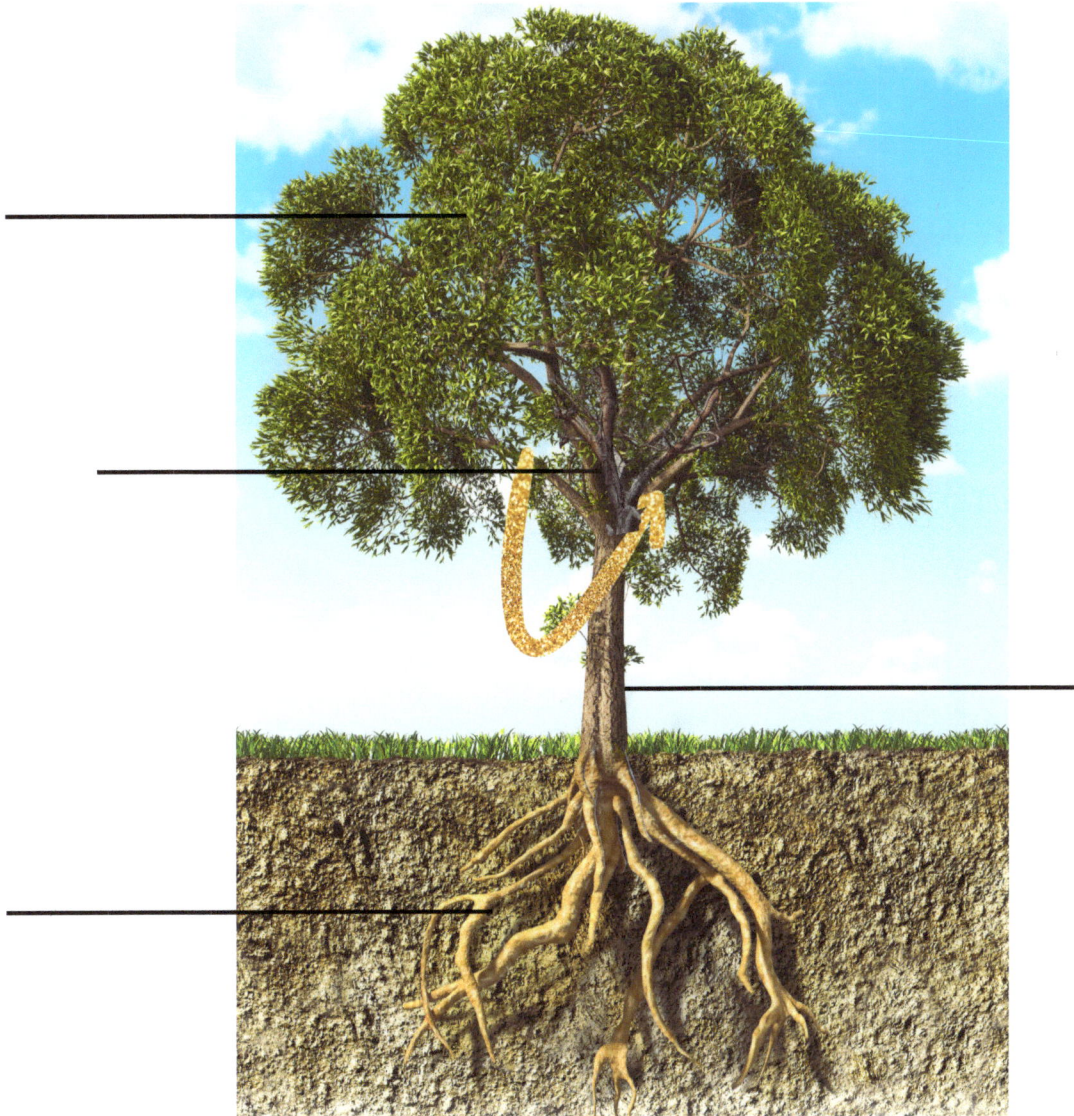

roots   **leaves**   **branches**   **trunk**

Draw a tree and label the parts

www.ingramcontent.com/pod-product-compliance
Lightning Source LLC
LaVergne TN
LVHW072117070426
835510LV00003B/105